BRITAIN'S HERITAGE

War Memorials

Roger Bowdler

AMBERLEY

Acknowledgements

I would like to thank Jonathan Black, Elizabeth Blood, Nicky Hughes and Jerry Young, Leo Schmidt, the late Gavin Stamp and Paul Stamper for their support in bringing this book to pass, and my editor, Nick Wright. My late brother Martin and late mother Jane have hovered over this project, while Christina, Basil and Iris have been present and correct.

Roger Bowdler

First published 2019

Amberley Publishing
The Hill, Stroud
Gloucestershire, GL5 4EP

www.amberley-books.com

Copyright © Roger Bowdler, 2019

The right of Roger Bowdler to be identified as the Author of this work has been asserted in accordance with the Copyrights, Designs and Patents Act 1988.

ISBN 978 1 4456 9101 5 (paperback)
ISBN 978 1 4456 9102 2 (ebook)

British Library Cataloguing in Publication Data.
A catalogue record for this book is available from the British Library.

Typesetting by Aura Technology and Software Services, India. Printed in the UK.

Contents

1
Introduction

Few other kinds of building or structure quite embody a nation's history as much as war memorials do. Ubiquitous and greatly varied, they tell the tale of international conflict, played out over centuries. Where did they come from? What were they for? How have they changed? These are some of the questions this book seeks to answer.

A war memorial is not a tomb, or a statue of a renowned commander. It is an object raised to keep the collective memory of fighting men in mind, and to perpetuate their names after death. So many soldiers, sailors and, later, airmen left for the wars: many never came back. Women served closer to the front in the First Word War, and in more recent times, in an age of total war, with the advent of aerial bombing, civilians have become victims too. Inscribing names on an enduring monument is one time-hallowed way of ensuring that these people escape oblivion. Inscriptions are at the heart of the reasons why memorials were erected, and the roll-calls they offer still provide a link with lost lives.

Today's notion of a war memorial tends to be shaped around the First World War: its aftermath heralded the greatest wave of monument-building Britain has ever seen, during which tens of thousands of memorials were erected, ranging from mighty statues to modest crosses. These memorials did not appear out of the blue; they were the upshot of a centuries-old commemorative theme devoted to honouring the valiant. For centuries, this meant paying tribute to the leaders.

Great Britain is proud of its naval and military heritage. Increasingly fostered in schools, a military ethos had been crucial in building a vast empire, and greater public respect was being paid to servicemen of all levels of the armed forces from the later Victorian period onwards. But Britain was not the first country to develop a tradition of local remembrance towards all who had died for their country, irrespective of rank. Germany (unified in 1871) had evolved a public mode of honouring its dead: local memorials had been erected to the fallen of the Wars of Liberation (1813–15), and the string of short wars in the 1860s, and especially the Franco-Prussian War of 1870–71, led to a spate of memorials, which in many ways anticipated Britain's memorials in their roll-calls of the dead.

The United States had endured a fearful Civil War from 1861 to 1865. Its commemorative tradition also anticipated Britain's in several ways. Not only did it produce a government-led approach to honouring the dead in national cemeteries and with uniform grave markers, it also saw the erection of many local war memorials, initially in Union-supporting areas, but later in Confederate ones too. France and Italy too had their own approaches. France raised memorials to the dead of Napoleon III's wars, while Italy honoured those who had died in the Risorgimento, the nation's unification. Martial Britain could thus look elsewhere to see new traditions of democratised military honour.

But just who qualified for remembrance? War memorials shed fascinating light on the way ordinary soldiers were perceived, and on how the State saw its duties towards those who had given their lives for the nation. It took a long time before an egalitarian approach emerged. Military leaders such as Marlborough, Wolfe, Nelson and Wellington received

Right: J. Moser's Memorial to the Franco-Prussian War, Naumburg (Germany). Erected after the Franco-Prussian War (1870–1), this monument features Germania in honour of the newly unified empire. The names of all of the dead are listed: a truly modern war memorial.

Below: Antietam National Cemetery, Maryland (USA). Opened in 1867, this state-funded burial ground contains the Union dead from the Battle of Antietam (1862). The Private Soldier Monument dates from 1880.

mighty tributes across the British Isles and beyond, and wealthier families preserved the memory of their dead through memorials, but the rank-and-file soldiers and sailors who secured their victories were largely ignored.

War memorials are found on very different scales. Mighty cities like Birmingham and Liverpool commissioned grand memorials which brought proud embellishment to their centres. Villages, on the other hand, could afford only modest monuments which tended to stick to tried and tested formulae: the cross, the obelisk or the plinth. Most were the products of the monumental mason, used to supplying family tombs to graveyard or cemetery. Others were more bespoke, the work of sculptors and architects who were given commissions to create one-off tributes to the dead. These memorials were raised to bring communities together in mourning: their unveilings were important events, and they continue to be at the centre of the rituals of remembrance.

Not all war memorials were raised to remember the dead of a place. Regiments, schools and colleges, companies and congregations, sporting teams and other associations each banded together to mark their own communities' losses. On the North Kent coast, one cement works commissioned a concrete statue of Victory. In London, the proud firm of

S. N. Cooke & W. N. Twist's Birmingham Hall of Memory (1925). One of the grandest civic memorials in Britain, it is built around a shrine-like casket containing a roll of honour: 12,320 citizens never came back from the fighting.

Francis Doyle-Jones' Bevan's War Memorial, Northfleet (Kent). Located in a cement works, this company memorial (made of cement) depicts Victory. The names of the dead also have their job titles.

Ferdinand Blundstone's Prudential Assurance Company Memorial, Holborn (London). Unveiled in 1922, this memorial stands in the core of the company's headquarters building. Angels escort the dying soldier to heaven. (Jerry Young)

the Prudential Assurance Company commissioned a dramatic bronze sculpture in 1921 from Ferdinand Blundstone, showing a dying man being received into Heaven by bare-breasted angels. It originally stood in the entrance courtyard of its imposing Gothic premises: every day, thousands of clerks and managers would pass the long lists of names of the fallen, and keep their dead colleagues in mind. It was meagre consolation for those left behind to mourn, but it was something, at least, to protect these names from oblivion. That is what a war memorial does. As historian Arnold Whittick wrote in his *War Memorials* (1946), 'The principal purpose of a memorial is to stir remembrance, and to keep alive and ever before us what is commemorated.'

During the First World War, Britain developed one of the most sophisticated programmes ever of State remembrance. The Imperial (and after 1960 the Commonwealth) War Graves Commission was founded in 1917. It aimed to afford dignified burial for all the nation's dead: where bodies were lost – and in the First World War, there was a strikingly high proportion of missing – the names would be recorded on group memorials. Dignity of design and equality in treatment were two of the hallmarks of this approach. This met with fierce resistance in some quarters, which the State overcame by putting the perpetuity of its mission before short-term family grief.

Local war memorials were a different matter. They were the fruits of individual committees and had no rulebooks to follow. In some places, local communities preferred practical memorials – a football stand, for instance, or a hospital extension – to a sculpted monument. This debate about the most fitting form of memorial was particularly heard after 1945, when there was even less appetite for monument-making. In most places, the dates of the Second World War could be added to those of the First, and the list of names updated. New bespoke memorials from the war of 1939–45 are far fewer in number, and generally modest in character.

Some people imagined that war memorials would slip from public consciousness as the decades separated the present from past conflicts. This has not happened. Indeed, there have been many high-profile memorial projects in recent years, which this short study will look at. It is a tribute to the potency of war memorials, and a reflection of the awfulness of the tragedy they embody, that interest in them today is as high as it has ever been. This book sets out to explain why this should be.

2

Ancient Heroes: Military Memorials Prior to 1700

Many ancient skeletons reveal clear evidence of combat-inflicted wounds, and burials with weapons and armour reveal the status accorded to the warrior in early society. Stonehenge's giant stones were embellished with over a hundred carvings of axe-heads and daggers in the early Bronze Age, indicative of the enduring prestige of military symbols. More is known about the military memorials of classical antiquity. Ancient Athenian monuments scrupulously recorded the names of citizens who fell for the nation, and earthen mounds (called a *soros* or *tymbos*) were raised as memorials over the battlefield graves of the slain: whether any British barrows mark any such clashes is a matter for speculation.

Roman commemoration placed greater emphasis on triumph, rather than sorrow, and on the Emperor rather than the dead. Perhaps Britain's earliest military monument was the large marble-clad triumphal arch of *c*. AD 85 at Richborough (Kent), celebrating the Roman conquest of Britannia. Roman tombstones began to name individual soldiers from the first century AD: examples can be seen at Chester, Gloucester, Wroxeter and Colchester.

Early medieval carved stones sometimes depicted fighting. At Lindisfarne, on the Northumberland coast, a ninth-century grave marker shows seven warriors brandishing weapons. Anglo-Saxon literature celebrated valour: the battle of Maldon (Essex) of 993, England's earliest securely identified battlefield location, inspired a verse epic which described English valour in the face of a Viking incursion. Particularly intriguing is the so-called Sueno's Stone, Scotland's tallest early medieval carved monument, at Forres (Moray). Dated to the tenth century, it is thought by some to mark the victory of Christian Gaels over pagan Picts, and by others the death in 966 of Dub mac Maíl Coluim (or Duff McMalcom), King of Alba. Its reliefs depict battle scenes, with dense ranks of

Sueno's Stone, Forres (Moray). Scotland's tallest Pictish sculpture probably dates from the tenth century. Its reliefs show battle scenes and a mass beheading. The monument is now protected by a glass shelter. (From a mid-twentieth-century postcard)

Battle Abbey, Battle (East Sussex). William the Conqueror founded a Benedictine Abbey on Senlac Hill, the scene of the Battle of Hastings (1066). The high altar stood on the spot where King Harold was slain. (From a 1906 postcard, showing the gatehouse)

Battlefield Church, Shrewsbury (Shropshire). The church of St Mary Magdalene originated after the Battle of Shrewsbury (1403). With the support of the victor, Henry IV, a local priest founded this collegiate church to say prayers for the souls of the dead. (Paul Stamper)

spear-toting warriors, and a depiction of decapitated bodies, as well as an enthronement: this narrative sequence, yet to be fully decoded, is highly expressive of the drama of war, and of the social consequences of its outcome.

The greatest military narrative cycle of the Middle Ages is surely the Bayeux Tapestry. Embroidered soon after William of Normandy's conquest of England in 1066, its detailed depictions of fighting, and of the dead, reveal a fascination with the depiction of warfare. William's foundation of Battle Abbey on Senlac Hill, the traditional location of King Harold's array, was one of the first certain English war memorials. Founded in about 1071 as a Benedictine abbey, it was an act of atonement for the blood spilt during the Conquest; the high altar was situated over the very spot on which Harold was said to have been slain. A later example of this preoccupation with posthumous remembrance can be found in the Welsh Marches. After the Battle of Shrewsbury (Shropshire, 1403), a church was built over a mass grave in order that prayers could be said for the dead: the village which grew around this is still known as Battlefield. Other fields of conflict were marked through the erection of crosses: Towton, England's bloodiest battlefield, features one such within its bleak landscape, a godly memorial to all of the slain even if it is now called by the name of one of the most prominent of the casualties – Dacre's Cross, after Ralph, Lord Dacre.

Funerary portraits in churches of armed knights became common in the High Middle Ages. From the thirteenth century onwards, these armoured effigies proliferated: first as recumbent stone effigies, and then in brass. Their heyday coincided with the Hundred Years War (1337–1453). Some of these men may have died fighting: one such example is the alabaster effigy of Lionel, Lord Welles at Methley (West Yorkshire), who was killed at the Battle of Towton (1461). Another fatal casualty of the Wars of the Roses (this time slain at the Battle of Barnet, in 1471) was Sir Humphrey Bourchier, who was buried beneath a (now-lost) brass effigy in St Edmund's Chapel, Westminster Abbey. His Latin epitaph, translated, includes precocious references to the human cost of warfare: 'Behold lying here the warrior at Barnet, eager for fierce fights; he fights like Eacides [i.e. Achilles]; the knight is wounded on all sides; he falls smitten; Mars brings him a wound; his armour spattered with blood grows red. Lo, the tearful grief of the hour. He falls, indeed, from the light, whither Christ rose from the dead... once this man was distinguished in arms and dear to Britons; ask in your prayers that he may live in heaven.' Some of the key themes of the war memorial – pride in martial renown, and sadness – are clearly present here.

Did you know?

All Souls' College, Oxford, was founded in 1434 by Henry Chichele, Archbishop of Canterbury, and Henry VI, both as a personal foundation and as an early form of war memorial. Prayers needed to be said for the souls of the legion dead of the Hundred Years War, many of whom had not died in a state of grace as fighting had prevented them from making their preparations to God. The college entrance sports a 1930s version of a relief, showing the resurrection of the dead.

All Souls College, Oxford. The sculpture over the entrance, shows the resurrection of the dead above a skeleton. The college was founded in 1438 by Archbishop Henry Chichele, partly in memory of the dead of the Hundred Years War.

The monument of Edward St John (1617–45), Lydiard Tregoze (Wiltshire). A Royalist cavalry officer, he was fatally wounded at the Second Battle of Newbury (1644). The 'Golden Cavalier' is the most renowned memorial to a victim of the Civil War.

Nonetheless, regarding medieval knightly effigies as an early form of war memorial, or even as portraits of fighting men, is problematic. These were first and foremost monuments of social status and piety, reserved for monarchs, aristocrats and the knightly class. Stained glass was sometimes used to commemorate great men, too. The celebrated east window at Gloucester Cathedral dates from *c.* 1350, and its figures include a number of knights, representing the commanders who served under Edward III in the Crécy-Calais campaign of 1346–7, including Sir Maurice de Berkeley, who never returned from France.

Armoured effigies continued after the Reformation: few of their subjects ever fought on campaign, however. Towards the end of the sixteenth century, the fighting in the Low Countries against Catholic forces drew in British participants. The north transept of Westminster Abbey contains several large tombs to some of the commanders, including Lord Norris (d. 1601) and Sir Francis Vere (d. 1609): very military in character, including scenes of fighting, they embody a new awareness of the display of valour.

The English Civil War (1642–51) brought this fighting home. However, there are few church monuments to its casualties, let alone to the rank and file. One of the most renowned is at Lydiard Tregoze (Wiltshire), commemorating Edward St John, who died of wounds received at the Second Battle of Newbury (1644). Beneath his gilded statue is a relief of St John leading his cavalry troop. There are echoes here of a new interest in classical modes of honouring the valiant, and the beginnings of a desire to mark, publicly, the memory of those killed in battle. During the Interregnum, monuments were raised in Westminster Abbey to some of the principal commanders of the Parliamentarian cause: to Oliver Cromwell (1599–1658) and his son-in-law, Henry Ireton (1611–52). These were destroyed after the Restoration, in 1660. One other, to Colonel Edward Popham (*c.* 1610–51), is still in the Abbey, with his armoured effigy standing alongside his wife. In a Restoration act of *damnatio memoriae* (a Roman practice, involving the removal of inscriptions referring to disgraced persons), his epitaph was removed. Monuments combine words and images: to remove one aspect is to deprive them of much of their force, and to lose the sense of identity that an inscribed name bestows.

3
Admirals and Generals: The Age of Great Commanders 1700–1840

Public monuments began to increase in number from the late seventeenth century. When a giant column was erected in the City of London to mark its recovery from the ravages of the Great Fire of 1666, designed by Sir Christopher Wren and Robert Hooke, it was called simply 'The Monument' as it had no rivals. Thereafter, statues, arches and obelisks began to appear across the face of the land. This tendency to raise monuments coincided with Britain's emergence as a naval, military and economic power. Triumphs were increasingly celebrated along Roman lines, using classical forms to celebrate these achievements, and as in the Roman culture of honour, the laurels were chiefly reserved for the figureheads, with national prestige being embodied in the sovereign.

Victory and heroism were the themes of these kinds of martial memorial: remembrance and gratitude for the sacrifices of the fighting forces were not yet considerations in the framing of the Georgian military monument. Not that monarchs were indifferent to the sufferings of fighting men: Charles II founded the Royal Hospital, Chelsea (established in 1681), expressly to house wounded veterans 'broken by age and war'. Its even grander naval equivalent, Greenwich Hospital, was founded in 1692 on the direction of Mary III after seeing the sufferings endured by casualties from the Battle of La Hougue. Its palatial main chamber, the Painted Hall, contains a triumphal mural cycle celebrating Protestant Great Britain's naval pre-eminence. Compassion for the wounded underpinned these royal foundations (as it had that of the Kilmainham Hospital, Dublin, opened in 1684), but there was no place in these institutions for remembrance of the dead.

In the early eighteenth century, few figures better embodied the cult of the hero better than John Churchill, Duke of Marlborough (1650–1722). He came to European notice for his serial victories over France and her allies in the War of Spanish Succession (1701–14): a grateful nation rewarded him with a grand royal estate and by building him the lavish Blenheim Palace (Oxfordshire), named after his greatest victory. Sir John Vanbrugh's Baroque design incorporated vast stone grenades in its ornamentation and a massive bust of his principal foe, Louis XIV, on its façade. The Victory Column, a giant Corinthian pillar which stands in the parkland, supporting a lead statue of Marlborough dressed as a Roman emperor, stood on a massive plinth bearing long inscriptions about his achievements. Landscaped parks were ideal locations for monuments. At Stowe (Buckinghamshire), several with martial overtones were erected by the Lords Cobham. Captain Grenville's Column paid tribute to a family member who had been fatally wounded at the First Battle of Finisterre (1747), and consisted of a rostral column firmly based on Roman models. A Latin inscription

Left: Henry Herbert, 9th Earl of Pembroke, is memorialised by the Column of Victory, Blenheim Palace (Oxfordshire). Raised in 1730–1, its base featured lengthy inscriptions detailing Marlborough's triumphs and the details of his rewards from a grateful Queen Anne and parliament.

Below: The Grenville Column, Stowe (Buckinghamshire). Captain Thomas Grenville was fatally wounded during the First Battle of Finisterre (1747). This *columna rostrata* was based on ancient Roman naval monuments which displayed the prows of captured enemy ships.

added in 1757 quoted his dying words, and stated: 'May this noble instance of Virtue prove instructive to an abandoned Age, and teach Britons how to act in their Country's Cause!' Private landscapes were the most appropriate places in which to explore new ways of using monuments to express messages to posterity.

The mid-eighteenth century also witnessed the erection of the first ever state-funded public memorial to a hero. It took the form of a large church monument in the nation's premier place of honour, Westminster Abbey. Captain James Cornewall was killed at the Battle of Toulon (1744). He was one of the few heroes of the fight, which saw the Spanish Navy scatter the British line of ships; Cornewall's HMS *Marlborough* had been in the thick of the fighting, and whereas other captains were court-martialled for a want of ardour, his reputation soared. That he had also been a Member of Parliament helped his case too. In 1749, a memorial designed by (Sir) Robert Taylor was installed in Westminster Abbey in his honour. Ten years later, the death of General James Wolfe at Quebec created a new kind of

The monument to Captain James Cornewall RN (d. 1744), located in the Westminster Abbey cloisters. Unveiled in 1749, this was the first publicly funded memorial raised to a hero. (By courtesy of the Dean and Chapter of Westminster)

William Wilkins' Nelson Column at Great Yarmouth (Norfolk), dating from 1817–20. Topped by a giant statue of Britannia, this memorial erected in the county of Nelson's birth also served as a navigational marker. (From a 1910 postcard)

Lord Hill's Column, Shrewsbury (Shropshire). Designed by Edward Haycock Senior, this memorial to Wellington's comrade-in-arms was built in 1814–16. It was raised during his lifetime (Hill died in 1842). (Engraving after T. H. Shepherd, c. 1845)

national hero. Prime Minister William Pitt the Elder led the call for a public monument, and an imposing memorial by Joseph Wilton was duly erected in 1772: this showed an angel lowering a laurel wreath towards the dying general, with a detailed bronze relief below showing the celebrated assault on the Heights of Abraham, which ensured victory and secured Canada for Britain.

Did you know?

Instead of raising grand monuments after 1815, and in the face of economic difficulties, the state response to commemoration was to divert funds into building new churches for the growing cities. Four of these, in South London, are known as the Waterloo Churches.

The posthumous public honouring of fallen heroes stepped up dramatically during the period of the French Revolutionary and Napoleonic Wars (1793–1815). Between 1794 and 1823, thirty-six monuments to military leaders (and a few statesmen) were erected, mainly in Saint Paul's Cathedral in London, at a cost of over £117,000. All were executed by leading sculptors in a Neoclassical style, in a consistent idiom which won for them the collective label of 'the Peninsular School'. A 'Committee of Taste' was established to select the rival designs for these prestigious commissions, and to ensure that they conformed to a certain

C. R. Cockerell and William Playfair's National Monument of Scotland, located at Calton Hill, Edinburgh. Begun in 1826, work on this version of the Parthenon halted in 1829, when funds dried up. It was subsequently called 'Scotland's Disgrace'.

approach which fused allegory and realism, classical mythology and military detail. Only the dead from upper ranks – from captains upwards for the Royal Navy, or colonels for the army – were entitled to such tributes: lower ranks could only play supporting roles on the monuments, and none were named. Admiral Lord Nelson's memorial by John Flaxman, unveiled in 1819, fourteen years after his death at Trafalgar, is an outstanding example of the genre. Nevertheless, these were the closest Georgian Britain got to the modern concept of war memorials and together they constitute a group of military tributes unsurpassed anywhere in Europe.

Various grandiose schemes for architectural victory memorials were hatched, but few saw the light of day. These put national triumph before a sense of human tragedy, and sought to aggrandise the city scene (particularly London's) with imposing structures. In 1799 the noted sculptor John Flaxman conceived of a colossal statue of Britannia, 230 feet high, to be raised on Shooter's Hill at Greenwich. Another fanciful scheme in 1815 wanted to cover the newly conceived public space of Trafalgar Square with an even taller pyramid.

Nelson's death led to a cult of posthumous honour. Glasgow, Dublin, Liverpool and Birmingham all raised spectacular structures to him, with the best-known of all, William Railton's Nelson's Column in Trafalgar Square, only being completed in 1843. Great Yarmouth (Norfolk) boasts of one of the finest: a tall column, erected as a navigational aid

Sir Richard Westmacott's Achilles statue, Hyde Park (London). Unveiled in 1822, it was the outcome of a scheme hatched by aristocratic women, and was the largest statue cast in Britain up to that time. Its bronze came from captured French cannon.

as well as a tribute, crowned with a giant statue of Britannia. Army commanders were also honoured with equally tall structures which dominated the skyline. Lord Hill (1772–1842), one of Wellington's closest and most successful comrades in the Peninsular War, was the recipient of a monumental Doric column on the edge of Shrewsbury (Shropshire), which was erected during his lifetime.

When monuments did depart from the time-hallowed tradition of honouring the leaders alone, trouble could ensue. In Edinburgh, the National Monument of Scotland was first proposed in 1816, and in 1826 work began on what was intended to be a replica of the Parthenon in Athens, adjusted to depict modern warriors, situated on the top of Calton Hill. Its architects, C. R. Cockerell and William Playfair, were outstanding Neoclassicists, and, had this superbly sited temple been completed, overlooking the Scottish capital and the Firth of Forth, one of the finest military memorials in Britain would undoubtedly have resulted. Intended to be 'A Memorial of the Past and Incentive to the Future Heroism of the Men of Scotland', the cost of the memorial was put at £42,000. Even though this was almost certainly a severe under-estimation, only £16,000 was raised, and work was halted with only one end built. Playfair, in 1829, wrote to Cockerell that the project 'is come to a dead Halt ... a striking proof of the pride and poverty of us Scots'. The truth is that memorials to individual commanders were the accepted way to honour valour: a *national* memorial had an ambiguity, a lack of specificity about it which failed to capture the public imagination of 1820s Scotland.

Joseph Gott sculpted this monument to Colonel Edward Cheney, Gaddesby (Leicestershire). Cheney (1778–1848) of the Scots Greys had four horses killed beneath him at Waterloo. This dramatic statue originally stood in Gaddesby Hall. It was brought into the church in 1898.

Monument to Captain John Buchanan (d. 1815), Chester Cathedral. Buchanan, of the 16th Light Dragoons, fell at Waterloo. This Greek Revival memorial was raised by his mother.

A hundred years later, Scotland would erect a magnificent national memorial to its war dead at Edinburgh Castle, which more than makes up for this abortive project from the Napoleonic epoch.

Wellington himself was the dedicatee of one of the most remarkable monuments of the Napoleonic epoch: the statue of Achilles, in London's Hyde Park. Cast from captured French cannon, Sir Richard Westmacott's Achilles statue in London's Hyde Park was unveiled in 1822 on the anniversary of the Battle of Waterloo. It was the largest bronze statue cast in Britain up to that date. It was also the first public monument commissioned by women. Based on the renowned classical sculptures of Castor and Pollux in Rome, it depicted the great hero of the Trojan Wars. First conceived in 1814, it was the brain-child of a group of aristocratic women, eager to pay tribute to the victor of the Peninsular War. There was initial alarm at the warrior's total nudity: a secret ballot was held to determine whether a fig leaf should be added. One duly was.

Monuments were erected in churches to more junior officers too. Few are more dramatic than the equestrian monument to Colonel Edward Cheney (d. 1848) of the Scots Greys, at Gaddesby, Leicestershire: he came back from the fighting, but four horses died beneath him at Waterloo (1815). Officers who were killed abroad sometimes received church monuments in their memory. Captain John Buchanan of the 16th Light Dragoons was killed at Waterloo and is commemorated in Chester Cathedral with a striking Greek Revival memorial commissioned by his mother. Outdoor tombs were beginning to be erected to a wider range of person, but the low social status of common soldiers and sailors, and the financial hardships of army and navy widows, made churchyard memorials to the fallen extremely rare. Tombstones to veterans who died back home exist, and in some number, but for those who never returned from active service their fate was often oblivion.

Despite the valour displayed on the gundecks of Nelson's navy, or in the ranks of Wellington's troops, the memory of the fighting man was left to chance. The dead of Waterloo, with the exception of a few officers, were stripped and buried in unmarked mass graves. One sign of a growing respect for rank and file servicemen can be cited: in 1816 it was announced that all who had served in the Waterloo Campaign would be issued with a bronze medal. This was a portent of what was to come: the dawning of the modern war memorial.

4
The Age of Empire 1840–1914

The half century between the start of the Crimean War and the First World War witnessed a transformation in the place of the army in society, and the culmination of Britain's imperial dream. This profoundly affected attitudes to memorials.

The names of rank-and-file soldiers began to be recorded on regimental memorials from the 1840s, and it was from here that the true origins of the modern war memorial can be traced. As the British Empire expanded, so did an appreciation of the role played by soldiers and sailors in bringing this about. National pride in the overthrow of Napoleon, and in particular a heightened pride in the fighting record of the British Army (much of which was recruited in Scotland and Ireland), raised the prestige of the Services. There were wider social factors at work here too. The Great Reform Act of 1832 heralded the start of greater public participation in affairs of State: slowly, a more democratic outlook began to arise. Literacy was on the rise, which made the recording of names a more pressing duty with a wider audience. This, allied to a growing pious sentimentalism about burial generally, made matters of military memory all the more sensitive.

Britain avoided Continental fighting in the forty years after Waterloo, but there were still plenty of smaller conflicts prior to the outbreak of the Crimean War, in 1854. These were principally in Asia, and included campaigns in modern-day Afghanistan, Pakistan, China and India. Campaign medals started to be regularly issued from 1839, and regiments raised memorials back home to their casualties. Outside the Royal Hospital stands a tall granite obelisk, inscribed 1849, which lists all of the names of the fallen of the 34th Foot who fell at the Battle of Chilianwala in the Punjab Campaign of 1848–9. In Lichfield Cathedral, the dead of all ranks of the 80th Foot from the Sutlej Campaign of 1845–46 are also all named.

The Chilianwala Obelisk, Royal Hospital, Chelsea (London). Raised in 1852, this granite obelisk was erected in memory of the 34th Foot's service in the Punjab Campaign of 1848–9. It lists the names of the dead of all ranks, not just the officers.

Did you know?

It took sixty years for the Duke of Wellington's towering monument by Alfred Stevens in Saint Paul's Cathedral to be completed: he died in 1852, but only in 1912 did his tomb find its final position in the nave of the cathedral.

The funeral of the Duke of Wellington in 1852 witnessed the final great public outpouring of martial respect for one sole individual. From this point onwards, military memorials begin to assume their modern form: as tributes to all personnel, and not just the commanders.

In 1854, the outbreak of the Crimean War of 1854–56 saw Britain's first European conflict since the Napoleonic Wars. There were episodes of dogged valour, such as the Battle of Inkerman; incidents of reckless courage, such as the Charge of the Light Brigade; and above all there was the long, harsh and ultimately successful siege of Sebastopol. British casualties were heavy, made worse by poorly organised medical services. Many died of wounds and disease, at Scutari, and were buried in the soil of Britain's ally, Turkey. The public knew more about the actual conditions the army fought in, and how their wounded were cared for: William Russell's avidly read columns in *The Times* contributed to a greater domestic concern for the fighting man.

Matthew Noble's Crimean War memorial to the 77th (East Middlesex) Regiment, Saint Paul's Cathedral. The angel, fusing victory and life eternal, hovers in front of a scene of battlefield burial. The absence of the dead was increasingly sensed. (Saint Paul's Cathedral Archives)

The Guards' Crimean Memorial by John Bell, Waterloo Place, London (1861). Honour stands aloft, advancing laurel crowns to statues of guardsmen. The figures were cast from Russian cannon, taken at Sebastopol.

Crimean War memorial, Abbey Cemetery, Bath (1856). The dedication of this obelisk was watched by 15,000 people, and the event closed with a fireworks display. This is an early example of a local war memorial, naming all ranks of the city's fallen.

And unlike during the Napoleonic War, the absence of the dead started to be felt more widely, leading to a new sort of monument which kept the absent dead in mind.

London witnessed the most prominent of these, the earliest war memorials. The Guards Memorial in London's Waterloo Place pointed the way towards the future. Sculpted by John Bell, its bronze figures (cast from Russian cannon) represented heroic-scaled guardsmen beneath a figure of Victory. This was a monument to the élite Brigade of Guards, and it was forward-looking in depicting rank-and-file guardsmen and in honouring all ranks of dead. Another Neoclassical memorial to the Crimean War was the obelisk raised at Bath, in the Abbey Cemetery there; of the thirteen names listed, eight were officers – a reflection on the city's social make-up. The inscription is revealing: 'Erected by the Citizens of Bath, in honour under God, of those heroic men, especially their fellow citizens and friends here recorded, who laid down their lives in the campaigns of 1854–5, so triumphantly achieved for the liberties of Europe.' Local pride in their contribution to as high a goal as defending 'the liberties of Europe'. Smaller communities like Beeston (Nottinghamshire) began to raise memorials too: in this instance, a stone obelisk with inset marble panels detailing the town's four fatalities. Modest as it was, it was a precocious kind of local memorial in commemorating privates, not officers.

Prominently located outside Westminster Abbey stands the 1861 Westminster School Crimean and Indian Memorial. Designed by Sir George Gilbert Scott (1811–78), shortly to

Sir George Gilbert Scott's Westminster Scholars' Crimean War Memorial, Broad Sanctuary (London). Prominently located outside Westminster Abbey, this column, completed in 1861, was one of the first Gothic Revival war memorials.

become renowned as the architect of London St Pancras station and the Albert Memorial, it honoured alumni of the school who had served as officers, commencing with Field Marshal Lord Raglan, the commander-in-chief. It comprised a tall column topped with a statue of St George slaying the dragon, and bore the inscription ending 'in full assurance that the remembrance of their heroism in life and death will inspire their successors at Westminster with the same courage and self-devotion'. Memorials were not just retrospective tributes: they were erected to inspire future generations too, by appealing to impressionable pupils, eager for role models. Saint George, England's patron saint and a valiant fighter against evil, provided just the right Christian symbol.

After the neoclassicism of the Georgian period, the Victorians turned to the Gothic Revival. Scott was the leading architect of the Gothic Revival, and High Victorian memorials began to assume a specifically Christian character, deploying Gothic forms. 'Muscular Christianity' was one of the key ideologies behind the imperial mission, and its leading proponent, Charles Kingsley, encouraged Britain's fighting forces: in an 1855 sermon sent out to forces in the Crimea called *Brave Words for Brave Soldiers and Sailors* he stated 'whosoever fights in a just war, against tyrants and oppressors, he is fighting on Christ's side, and Christ is fighting on his side'. Regimental memorials were raised in Britain's cathedrals in considerable numbers

William Wailes' Northumberland Fusiliers Indian Mutiny window, Newcastle Cathedral. Made in a local studio, this characteristic Gothic Revival stained glass memorial was unveiled in 1861.

in the later Victorian period, often in the preferred Gothic Revival media of stained glass or brasses. The memorial window by William Wailes in Newcastle Cathedral to the fatalities of the Northumberland Fusiliers in the Indian Mutiny (1857–8) features Saint George slaying the dragon; names of all the dead are on a brass plaque beneath.

Major reforms to the organisation of the army took place under Prime Minister William Gladstone's administration, led by Edward Cardwell, Secretary of State for War in 1868–74. Prussia's crushing victory over France in 1870–1 showed the need for a modern, professional, fighting force. In response, several developments took place which affected the social perception of the army. For one, a much stronger connection between place and regiment was forged. In 1871, the Regulation of the Forces Act ushered in a new approach to recruiting: by creating 'regimental districts', units were given a depot base which reinforced local pride in their regiment. Cardwell's successor, Hugh Childers, introduced further reforms in 1881 which strengthened the connection between volunteer units and regulars, further strengthening the connections between communities and the army.

Memorial to Fred Hitch VC (d. 1913), Chiswick Cemetery (London). Private Hitch was one of the heroes of Rorke's Drift, the renowned engagement of the Anglo-Zulu War of 1879. This monument was raised by public subscription in 1913.

The unveiling of the Northumberland Boer War Memorial at Newcastle-upon-Tyne, 22 June 1908. This was one of the most imposing Boer War memorials, and honoured the 373 dead of the county's regiments. (From a 1908 postcard)

Twenty campaign medals were issued between 1850 and 1900, indicative of ongoing conflicts and an official desire to recognize arduous service. Few memorials were raised to the fallen in the Zulu War of 1879, one of Britain's sharpest setbacks in its Empire conflicts. One of the heroes of the fierce fight against the Zulus in 1879 at Rorke's Drift, Private Frederick Hitch VC (1856–1913) was given a private memorial in Chiswick Cemetery, paid for by a public fundraising campaign eager to celebrate this renowned imperial incident. It is indicative of changing attitudes that a private could now attract such notice.

By the 1880s, many of the cities of Western Europe and North America were beginning to fall prey to 'Statuemania' – the proliferation of public monuments which can be detected from the 1880s onwards, and which only came to an end with the completion of memorials to the First World War in the 1920s. It was above all the Second Boer War of 1899–1902 that prompted the emergence of the modern war memorial: a nation-wide series of locally raised monuments to the dead, which named the individual soldiers and sailors who had lost their lives on active service. This cultural phenomenon was the result of several factors: of the ascendancy of nationalism; of a growing popular historical consciousness; and of a civic desire to beautify the fast-expanding modern city. There was also a stronger social connection between soldier and civilian: 25,000 reservists gave up ordinary life to rejoin the ranks. Casualties, caused by disease as well as combat, were high, with over 22,000 British troops losing their lives. Although the war (eventually won against far smaller forces) highlighted the deficiencies of the British Army, and included some unchivalrous treatment of civilians, it nonetheless triggered an imperial surge of monument-building.

These memorials were sometimes very grand. Newcastle-upon-Tyne, a proud city with a large armaments and ship-building economy, raised a tall victory column, embellished with allegorical figures. Designed by local artist Thomas Eyre Macklin, its tapering octagonal shaft carries a winged figure of Victory, with sword and wreath; at its base, a draped female figure representing Northumbria holds a regimental standard and a palm. When unveiled in 1908, the mayor described it as 'a thing of beauty ... an incentive to all to put their country's claims as one of the first objects of their lives'. He may not have been pleased to learn that the memorial's nickname became 'the Dirty Angel'.

Above: Arthur Walker's Bury St Edmunds Boer War memorial (Suffolk), 1904. *'Vulneratus non victus'* – 'Wounded but not defeated' – reads the inscription. Resilient bravery was a quality often stressed in this sort of monument.
Left: Nathaniel Hitch's East Kent Boer War Memorial, Dane John Gardens, Canterbury (1904). As the children in the foreground show, such monuments embellished the public realm with a new kind of imperial statuary. (From a c. 1910 postcard)

Elsewhere, realistic depictions of the fighting man, by now clad in more practical khaki uniforms, and generally sporting big moustaches, became the norm. The emphasis here is very much on individual courage in combat. Martial aggression may be an essential attribute in the field, but for commemorative purposes soldiers were better shown in defensive modes, protecting comrades and displaying resolute courage. Adrian Jones (1845–1938), formerly a captain in the Royal Army Veterinary Service, designed several Boer memorials: the 1903 one to the Royal Marines on London's new processional route, The Mall, embodied these manly virtues in its tableau of defiance. Bury St Edmunds (Suffolk) raised a monument in 1904, honouring no fewer than 193 men from the county: like the Royal Marines monument, this too depicted a wounded but defiant soldier. In Dane John Gardens, Canterbury, an obelisk fronted by a bronze statue of a soldier wearing a slouch hat and bandolier commemorated the East Kent Regiment ('The Buffs') and the East Kent Yeomanry, 234 of whom died on campaign. Bedford's bronze Boer War soldier stands at the ready, his stance the embodiment of calm determination. Allegory was sometimes present (as at Worcester, where an angel holds the olive branch of victory over a determined soldier), and so was Christian symbolism, like the statue of Saint George within Huntingdon's canopied Boer War memorial) but the public appetite for reportage and its fascination with the new face of warfare made these idealised military portraits particularly popular. Not all Boer War memorials were of the monumental kind. In Winchester, a granite horse trough was erected 'In Memory of the Horses Killed in the South African War'.

Below left: Leon Joseph Chavalliaud's Bedfordshire Boer War memorial, The Embankment, Bedford (1904). Boer War memorials often included detailed depictions of the modern fighting man.
Below right: Memorial to French prisoners of war at Norman Cross (Cambridgeshire), 1914. This reconciliatory column was erected by the 'Entente Cordiale Society'. In 1990 it was knocked down: the eagle sculpture is a modern replacement. (Paul Stamper)

Did you know?

Liverpool Football Club's ground at Anfield includes an unofficial memorial: the 'Kop'. This Boer term for a steep hill alludes to the battle fought at Spion Kop in 1900, which nearly resulted in a British disaster. This gave its name to earthen mounds raised at the goal-end of football pitches; several other football grounds built themselves a 'Spion Kop' as a spectator facility.

Not all military memorials honoured the nation's own dead. French prisoners from the Revolutionary and Napoleonic Wars had been kept in grim conditions, on board hulks and in overcrowded depots. In 1869, the Admiralty erected a Gothic monument on St Mary's Island in the Medway Estuary on the site of a prisoner of war cemetery: this was relocated to Chatham (when the bodies were again disinterred in advance of an extension of the Chatham dockyard) in 1904. Its inscription is poignant: 'They were deprived of the consolation of closing their eyes / Among the countrymen they loved / but they have been laid in an honourable grave / by a nation which knows how to respect valour / And to sympathise with misfortune.' Similar sentiments informed the erection of other such reconciliatory monuments. In 1914, an eagle-topped column was raised at Norman Cross (Cambridgeshire) in memory of the 1,770 French prisoners of war who died while interned at this military depot from 1797 to 1814. French and American prisoners (from the war of 1812–13) who had died at Dartmoor Prison were also honoured with memorials erected in 1868 and 1928. These nations, formerly Britain's enemies, were shortly to become staunch allies in the greatest conflict then known: the First World War.

5
The First World War

Nearly 1 million Britons lost their lives in the First World War of 1914–18. Some 750,000 of these were from the British Isles, which endured a 12 per cent fatality rate among all who served. Other parts of the Empire made up the rest of this heart-rending tally. The sheer scale of loss, allied to a firmly established taste for statues and memorials, led to the greatest wave of remembrance ever seen in these lands. So widespread and so diverse were these tributes that, even a century on, no one quite knows how many war memorials there are. There was a hard-won victory to give thanks for; an important aspect of commemoration which can get overshadowed by an emphasis on grief. But with so many lives lost, remembrance had never been so necessary.

The commemorative response was truly multilayered, from the vast war cemeteries on the Western Front, to the private tributes constructed at home out of photographs and card. This survey of the vast topic of First World War memorials can only touch on key aspects. It begins with the national ways of remembering, and then explores memorials to military units; after this, the great city memorials are discussed, before looking at the more numerous local tributes.

Nationally, the Imperial War Graves Commission began with the efforts of former newspaper editor Fabian Ware (1869–1949). Eager to serve but too old to enlist, he joined the Red Cross in 1914. Soon struck by the inadequacy of provisions for marking the graves of the dead, he gained army support for the creation of the 'Graves Registration Unit', which kept proper records, and which soon had 'an extraordinary moral value to the troops in the field', in the words of Field Marshal Haig. Formalised as the Imperial War Graves Commission (IWGC) in May 1917, it co-ordinated an unprecedented programme of burial and memorialisation both at home and at the many theatres of war. It drew on the design skills of some of Britain's leading architects in formulating an approach based on dignity, equality, and classicism in design. Private memorials were banned, as was the return of the bodies of the fallen; both of these decisions, taken to enable an orderly consistency to flourish, caused deep unhappiness among mourners. Having lost their loved ones in the national cause, they struggled to accept how the state could deprive them of the right to determine how they should be commemorated.

A homogenous approach was adopted, which (broadly speaking) applied the same design solutions across the war cemeteries of the world. These were set out in a report by Sir Frederic Kenyon, Director of the British Museum and Artistic Adviser to the IWGC, in 1918. A standard headstone was designed by committee, employing a special typeface evolved by MacDonald Gill. The 'Cross of Sacrifice' by Sir Reginald Blomfield (1856–1942) introduced a Christian note in the otherwise non-denominational cemeteries, while the 'Stone of Remembrance' by Lutyens created an altar-like block inscribed 'Their name liveth for evermore', the text being chosen by Rudyard Kipling. The hundreds of thousands of missing were to be named on special memorials, and there was to be no difference between officers and men in posthumous honour. Seldom has a state-run programme of design been so successful in its aims.

In London's Whitehall, the Cenotaph by Sir Edwin Lutyens (1869–1944) became the focus for the country's grief. Meaning 'empty tomb', the Cenotaph was not originally

Sir Reginald Blomfield's Highgate School War Memorial, Highgate (North London). Erected at Blomfield's old school in 1921, this was a version of his 'Cross of Sacrifice', designed for the Imperial War Graves Commission and erected at many war cemeteries.

Above left: Sir Edwin Lutyens' Cenotaph, Whitehall (London). Modest in scale, this classically inspired pylon was unveiled in its final form in 1920. It is the national and imperial monument to the million dead of the First World War, and still the focus of commemoration. (Jerry Young)

Above right: Sir Edwin Lutyens, the Southampton Cenotaph (Hampshire). This version of the classic design, dedicated in 1920, is slightly more elaborate than the Whitehall original, and includes a depiction of a dead soldier on the top.

intended to be permanent. Its austere classical form, marked simply by wreaths, dates and the words 'THE GLORIOUS DEAD', worked because of its very restraint: there were simply too many dead to do anything other than generalise. When the scale of the Cenotaph is considered alongside some of the more grandiose schemes then being proposed, its modesty is all the more remarkable. It was approachable in scale, yet dignified, and its austerity had a welcoming receptiveness about it: a more specific, or allegorical approach would have channelled mourners' feelings along predetermined lines. Unsurprisingly, other places adopted it as their memorial too. Lutyens' Cenotaph was emulated across the globe: versions were erected in Hong Kong, Auckland, Ontario and Bermuda.

Did you know?

Lutyens' Cenotaph was originally built of plaster, canvas and wood as it was only intended to form a temporary marker for the 1919 Peace Parade. However, it proved so popular as a focus for national grief that a Portland stone replacement was erected in 1920, in time for the procession of the Unknown Warrior to Westminster Abbey.

In the same way, the most renowned single burial of the First World War also appealed because of its universality. This was the Tomb of the Unknown Warrior, laid to rest in Westminster Abbey in 1920 (on the same occasion as the unveiling of the permanent version of the Cenotaph). The unidentified body was removed from the deathly wastes of the Western Front and was given honoured burial among monarchs and the nation's greatest. He stood for the 517,000 missing men who did not even have a grave; whose bodies had been fragmented or swallowed up in the hellish conditions of static trench warfare in an age of artillery domination. 'Their name liveth for ever more' – Kipling's phrase had deep resonance for a conflict of annihilation. War memorials aimed to fill some of this void by at least ensuring that their names would survive into the future.

Wales had a national monument in Cardiff, and Northern Ireland its counterpart in Belfast, beside the City Hall; there was also an all-Ireland memorial in Dublin, designed by Lutyens. The Scottish National War Memorial was designed by Sir Robert Lorimer (1864–1929) beside Edinburgh Castle, its late Gothic grandeur a tribute to the heavy casualties borne by the country, and a delayed compensation after the disappointment of its scarce-begun Napoleonic antecedent. Finished in 1927, it emerged organically from the citadel's rock and the flank of the castle, and brought together the arts of architecture, sculpture, stained glass and lettering in one vivid and sustained tribute to the recent

Sir Robert Lorimer's Scottish National War Memorial, Edinburgh. Finished in 1927, this chapel replaced a barrack block on Castle Rock to become one of Britain's most intricate and powerful war memorials. It is a shrine to Scotland's heavy losses.

Above left: Sir Robert Lorimer's Royal Navy Memorial, Chatham (Kent). Unveiled in 1924, this was one of three similar memorials at English naval bases to the 8,500 sailors lost at sea. (Jerry Young)
Above right: Adrian Jones' Gloucestershire Hussars War Memorial, Gloucester Cathedral Close. This cross, dedicated in 1922, is of note for its four relief plaques depicting this Territorial unit's service in the Near East.

conflict. Christian iconography jostles with reportage: scenes of medieval history coexist with depictions of weaponry and a tribute to 'The Tunnellers' Friends' – mice and caged birds. Lorimer was also the designer of the three memorials to the 8,500 missing of the Royal Navy, at Chatham, Portsmouth and Plymouth. Each comprises a stone shaft, surmounted by a bronze sphere carried on statues of the four winds and guarded by Lorimer's signature sentinel lions. The youngest branch of the services, the Royal Air Force, was only formed in April 1918. Its monument, located on London's Victoria Embankment, was designed by another IWGC architect, Sir Reginald Blomfield, and it took the form of a huge eagle upon another sphere. Sir William Reid Dick was its sculptor.

   The bond of comradeship was a strong one, and numerous regiments commissioned memorials. Some took traditional forms, such as Adrian Jones's monument to the Gloucestershire Hussars: a cross, erected in 1922 in the Gloucester Cathedral close, with reliefs of their campaigns in the Near East. Jones's Cavalry Memorial in Hyde Park, unveiled in 1924, showed a mounted Saint George raising his sword above a slain dragon. This taste for medieval imagery influenced many other memorials: that to the Territorial Battalion of the Northumberland Fusiliers in Newcastle is one of the finest. The same regiment's principal monument is the celebrated group sculpture by Sir William Goscombe John (1860–1952), called 'The Response', showing the city's volunteers marching to war in 1915, and taking leave of their families. Unusually, this was paid for by a wealthy ship-owner, partly in gratitude for the safe return of his five sons. Goscombe John's other great memorial is at Port Sunlight, and was equally ambitious in scale and figural drama.

Other formations opted for artistically progressive monuments. They included the largest unit in the British Army: the Royal Artillery. Having commissioned a rather conventional Boer War monument, the Gunners opted for a more adventurous tribute to their 49,045 fallen comrades. The architect Lionel Pearson, working with the rising sculptor Charles Sargeant

John Reid's war memorial to the 6th Battalion, Northumberland Fusiliers, at Saint Thomas's Church, Barras Bridge, Newcastle-upon-Tyne (1924). Numerous memorials featured knightly images of Saint George.

Above: Sir William Goscombe John's memorial to the Northumberland Fusiliers at Barras Bridge, Newcastle-upon-Tyne. Known as 'The Response', this 1923 memorial is one of the largest to any unit, and was the gift of local ship-owner Sir George Renwick. The inclusion of civilians is unusual.

Right: Sir William Goscombe John's Port Sunlight War Memorial (Merseyside). Unveiled in 1921, this ambitious war memorial stands at the heart of the model settlement built for the employees of Lever Brothers, soap manufacturers.

Lionel Pearson and Charles Sargeant Jagger's Royal Artillery Memorial, Hyde Park Corner (1924). One of the most powerful memorials of all, its uncompromising depiction of modern warfare displayed Jagger's extensive front line experience. (Jerry Young)

Jagger (1885–1934), produced a daring design which featured a 9.2-inch howitzer, realised in Portland stone. On the sides of the plinth were heroic-scaled bronze statues of artillerymen, between reliefs showing the modern realities of the gunner's war: Jagger had won the Military Cross for bravery. The First World War was emphatically a conflict dominated by artillery: over 70 per cent of combat casualties were inflicted this way.

The Royal Artillery Memorial is also renowned for its depiction of the dead. Limehouse's memorial showed a scene of a blasted trench, strewn with bodies, while others depicted the allegorical dead being received into celestial realms.

Even more daring was the selection of the painter Eric Kennington (1888–1960), untried in sculpture, to execute the memorial to the 24th Division. A trio of Tommies, holding comradely hands, stands on a pedestal with unit badges; African influence is clearly sensed in their heads. One unit memorial was long misunderstood. This was the 1925 Machine Gun Corps Memorial by Francis Derwent Wood (1871–1926), which juxtaposed a nude figure of David between two Vickers machine guns; how could so pitiful and irrelevant a contrast be permitted? Recent research has shown that Wood's war service in a hospital, working on prosthetic masks for the disfigured, made him more aware than anyone of the impact of shell and bullet on the human form: David's bodily beauty is the whole point of the

Above: Charles Sargeant Jagger's Royal Artillery Memorial, showing detail of a dead gunner. Such bold depictions of the dead were extremely unusual.

Below: A. G. Walker's Limehouse Memorial War Memorial (East London). This relief, unveiled in 1921 beneath a statue of Christ, included a grim scene of bodies in a trench. It was repeated upon Shrewsbury School's 1923 memorial.

Above left: Sir Thomas Brock and F. Arnold Wright's Queen's University Belfast War Memorial (1924). Such depictions of the dead being borne heavenwards made manifest ideas of enduring memory and honour.

Above right: Eric Kennington's 24th Division war memorial in Battersea Park, South London (1924). Artistically progressive for its day, the memorial shows the influence of African sculpture. One of the models was the celebrated poet and memoirist Robert Graves. (Jerry Young)

memorial, besides being a tribute to undaunted valour. Another unusual memorial is the 1920 sculpture modelled by Cecil Brown, raised in memory of the men of the Imperial Camel Corps who perished in Egypt and Palestine.

Britain's great cities erected fitting monuments to reflect the scale of their losses, and to express pride in victory. A sense of departure and homecoming formed the theme of the Liverpool Cenotaph. Designed by Lionel Budden (1877–1956) and featuring sculptural reliefs by Henry Tyson Smith (1883–1972), it stood in the shadow of St George's Hall, close to the city's ceremonial heart. On one side, ranks of men march off to war; on the other, an unparalleled scene of mourning is represented as civilians visit one of the war cemeteries. The war had not been a matter of fighting alone: all of society had been drawn into its lethal orbit. Unveiled in 1930, its deep sadness suggests the anti-war feeling that was beginning to find expression.

Some elected to represent the particular spirit of place in their monument. Loughborough (Leicestershire) is renowned for its bell-casting industry. Accordingly, the town erected a carillon – a tall bell tower – in Queen's Park and commissioned the elderly Sir Edward Elgar to compose a special tune to be played on the set of forty-seven bells, creating a unique sonic memorial to the dead. Inside is another novel feature: a war museum.

Above left*:* Cecil Brown's Imperial Camel Corps War Memorial, Victoria Embankment Gardens (London). Unveiled in 1920, this brought the drama of desert warfare home to the heart of the capital. Brown had also served on the Palestine Front. (Jerry Young)
Above right*:* Lionel Budden and Henry Tyson Smith's (sculptor) Liverpool Cenotaph, Saint George's Plateau, Liverpool. Completed in 1930, this outstanding memorial bore two long reliefs of men marching to war, and civilians grieving at a war cemetery.

Smaller communities sometimes opted for a memorial which embodied the essence of a local place. Using local stone could achieve this. At Lelant (Cornwall), an elemental construction of huge granite blocks made an enduring tribute to the dead, while at Blair Atholl (Perth and Kinross) a giant stone of remembrance, inscribed '1914 – 1918', was raised, close to a memorial park. The sheer time-depth of this geological tribute was an eloquent expression of the desire to perpetuate memories of the dead: 'Lest we forget' is the purpose of a monument after all.

Did you know?

The Commondale Shepherds War Memorial on the North Yorkshire Moors, west of Whitby, remembers two local shepherds who enlisted together in the Grenadier Guards. Neither returned. This granite post, one of the remotest memorials anywhere, marks their favourite spot.

Sir Walter Tapper's Loughborough Carillon Tower (Leicestershire). Opened in 1923, this memorial reflects the town's specialist industry: bell-founding. Elgar composed a piece specially for the unveiling, played on its forty-seven bells. (Elizabeth Blood, postcard of c. 1925)

The war memorial at Lelant, Cornwall. Made of local granite, the massive forms of this monument drew on the area's geology and building traditions.

Above left: The Stone of Remembrance at Blair Atholl (Perth and Kinross). Unveiled by the Duke of Atholl in 1924, this massive memorial of local stone stressed the enduring nature of remembrance of the dead. (Jerry Young)

Above right: Gilbert Ledward's statue of Britannia in the Stockport War Memorial Art Gallery (Greater Manchester, 1925). Improving the lives of citizens while remembering the dead was a common aim, but memorial art galleries were most unusual.

Some urban memorials served other purposes, besides purely commemorative ones. Stockport's elaborate memorial incorporated an art gallery, its vestibule embellished with inscriptions around a powerful statue by Gilbert Ledward depicting Britannia and a naked, dying man. Public parks were another means of achieving the same end – of using the sacrifice of the fallen as a way towards a better life for the survivors. Carlisle purchased open land and built a memorial bridge to reach it; Worcester celebrated an episode of great bravery its local regiment had demonstrated during the First Battle of Ypres (1914) by opening a new open space called Gheluvelt Park, overlooked by housing for disabled ex-servicemen. Even before the Armistice, Cleethorpes started to plan for a new civic complex which was to include exercise areas, music venues, youth clubs and other facilities for the young. The small Somerset town of Wiveliscombe was one of several communities to open a football stadium (with grandstand) in memory of its dead. Some communities channelled funds into more essential facilities, such as hospital wards or school buildings. The London Borough of Islington, which contained many areas of deprivation, put the funds raised for remembrance towards a large extension of the Great Northern Hospital; this explains the extreme modesty of the concrete post on Islington Green which (until 2009, when a new memorial by John Mayne RA was installed) constituted the borough's focus of commemoration.

Above: Grandstand at Wiveliscombe War Memorial Recreation Ground (Somerset; 1920). The war dead had been young men: facilities which benefited future generations of youth were popular with many communities. (Paul Stamper)

Left: John Maine's Islington War Memorial, Islington Green (North London). Completed in 2007, this is one of the most ambitious of new memorials to localities. It replaced a plain concrete structure, erected in 1918. Islington's main memorial had been an extension to the Great Northern Hospital.

Even more local were the street shrines and memorials. These began life during the war as temporary tributes to serving men, and as news of fatalities reached home, they became public memorials. Bethnal Green, in London's East End, had a number (one survival is to be seen in Cyprus Street), and at New Court in Hampstead a small aedicule was installed, naming the men who had left these blocks of flats to fight; those who did not return were marked with a cross. St Albans (Hertfordshire) launched a scheme for memorial street signs, which named the dead in the roads they had lived in.

Village crosses and obelisks were the most common kind of rural memorial. Some were simple structures, listing names, while others took more intricate forms. One such is at Leckhampstead (West Berkshire), where the obelisk has a clock face, the hands made from bayonets and the hours marked by bullets; it stands inside a chain, salvaged from a ship which fought at Jutland (1916) and suspended from shell cases. Another unusual village memorial is at Westwell (Oxfordshire). It is a gnarled shaft of local stone, embellished with one of the bronze characters from the clock face of the Cloth Hall at Ypres, one of the great medieval monuments to be destroyed in the fighting. Village crosses could attain

Above left: New Court War Memorial, Hampstead (North London). This tablet marks the sacrifice made by two blocks of artisan dwellings. Of the fifty who fought, ten were killed – nearly twice the national average loss rate.

Above right: Leckhamstead War Memorial (West Berkshire). This detail shows the clock face on the obelisk, decorated with bayonets and bullets. Incorporating relics into memorials was very rare. (Jerry Young)

Above left: F. L. Griggs' Snowshill War Memorial (Gloucestershire). Unveiled in 1923, this represents the enduring inspiration of medieval memorial crosses. Griggs' deep understanding of medieval and Cotswolds traditions is evident in its elegant design. (Elizabeth Blood)

Above right: Eric Gill's Trumpington War Memorial (Cambridgeshire; 1921). The base shows Saint George slaying the dragon: he wears a steel helmet, fusing modernity and traditional symbolism. This is among the most renowned of war memorial crosses.

exquisite quality: at Snowshill in the Cotswolds, the artist F. L. Griggs designed one such, reviving a medieval tradition: an organisation was founded to promote more. One of the finest war memorial crosses is at Trumpington, just south of Cambridge. On it, Eric Gill (1882–1940) carved religious scenes at its base, fusing biblical imagery with depictions of the Tommy.

Landscape memorials exist on a number of scales. Extensive areas were given to the National Trust in memory of the dead, including Scafell in the Lake District: one of thirteen summits given by the Fell and Rock Climbing Club. At Whipsnade (Bedfordshire) a 'Tree Cathedral' was planted in 1931, laid out like a cathedral, in memory of fallen friends; memorial trees were quite common ways of creating living memorials. Outside Brighton an Indian memorial stands within the South Downs, marking where soldiers who died of wounds had been cremated at a *chattri*. Memorials on hilltops dominated the landscape, and ensured that the dead were kept in mind in the land they had come from.

Right: The *Chattri* Memorial, Patcham (East Sussex). Fifty-three Hindu and Sikh soldiers who died of wounds in 1914–15 were cremated on this spot: the Prince of Wales unveiled this Indian-inspired memorial in 1921. (Jerry Young)

Below: Stockdale, Harrison & Sons' Leicestershire Yeomanry War Memorial, Bradgate Park (1927). This obelisk of cement occupies a commanding position with extensive views over a notable historic landscape just outside Leicester.

Suburbs too could commemorate. At Purley, South East London, a smart suburban development of 1923 included a tree-lined route called the Promenade de Verdun: an avenue of poplars, planted in soil from a French battlefield, led to a memorial to the fallen French. Another community which erected memorials was the workplace. These could range from the great railway companies to small enterprises, and from banks to museums. The

Did you know?

Knowlton in Kent has a memorial column designed by Sir George Frampton (1860–1928), sculptor of *Peter Pan* in Kensington Gardens. This was raised in 1915 after *The Weekly Despatch* launched a competition to find the nation's bravest village. Out of total population of thirty-nine, twelve had enlisted. All returned, making Knowlton one of the 'Thankful Villages'.

London & South Western Railway was still building its London terminus at Waterloo when war broke out: its principal entrance became the Victory Arch, embellished with much architectural sculpture depicting '1914', '1918' and Victory. The Great Western Railway opted for a single figure, which has become one of the most admired of all memorial sculptures: Jagger's *The Letter*. Smaller firms raised memorials too: the Daniell brewery at

The Victory Arch, Waterloo station (South London). Executed for the London & South Western Railway's newly built London terminus, this *Beaux Arts* composition of 1920–22 showed Britannia triumphant, flanked by allegorical groups of *1914* and *1918*.

Charles Sargeant Jagger's Great Western Railway memorial at Paddington station, London (1922). This poignant monument on Platform 1 of the station shows a Tommy, wrapped for winter warfare, reading a letter from home.

Memorial to the victims of the Faversham munitions factory disaster, Faversham Cemetery (Kent). Sparks from a chimney ignited a pile of sacks, resulting in a huge explosion in April 1916: 108 men and boys are buried beneath this monument.

West Bergholt (Suffolk) had a ceramic roll-call of the fallen inside its offices. Shops erected war memorials: for example, the famous Liberty's store in London has a wooden name board on its main staircase.

War production could be very dangerous. The worst civilian disaster of the war occurred at Chilwell, Nottinghamshire, when 139 were killed in an explosion in a munitions factory; a pyramidal memorial was erected over the mass graves in Attenborough churchyard. A similar catastrophe took place in April 1916 when 108 were killed at a munitions factory just north of Faversham, in the Kent marshes. A large cross was later erected above their mass graves.

Churches contain memorials to congregations and to individuals. They could consist of monuments or stained glass windows, or liturgical fittings like rood screens or altars.

Did you know?

In 1919, a Mark IV tank arrived in Saint George's Square, Ashford (Kent). It is still there, the only remaining example of such a war memorial. It escaped the Second World War scrap drive as it had been adapted to become an electricity substation.

Private memorials (generally to officers) could take either form. Lieutenant-Colonel Hugh Hill was killed in the Battle of the Somme: his stained glass memorial depicted modern scenes of trench warfare and his place of burial. The funeral effigy tradition found its last great expression in Eric Kennington's effigy at Wareham of T. E. Lawrence (d. 1935). Not strictly a war memorial, this is still a military portrait, recalling his heroic service in the deserts of Arabia.

Right: All Saints Church, Allhallows (Kent). This war memorial comprises a stained glass window depicting Saint George and the dragon (c. 1920). The crucifix and blood-red sky stress the sacrifice made by the parish dead.

Below: A. K. Nicholson Studio's memorial window to Lieutenant-Colonel Hugh Hill DSO (d. 1916) at Holy Trinity, Penn (Buckinghamshire). This memorial depicted the Black Prince and Joan of Arc, from the Hundred Years War; this panel shows British and French forces fighting together on the Somme.

Above: Eric Kennington's effigy of T. E. Lawrence at St Martin's Church, Wareham (Dorset; 1936–9). Lawrence of Arabia died in 1935 and is depicted in his Arab clothing, alluding to his distinguished war service in the desert. This is the last great military effigy.

Left: Herbert Baker's Winchester College War Memorial Cloister, Winchester (Hampshire; 1922–24). The finest school war memorial, this was designed to inspire future generations of Wykehamists with the concept of sacrifice and devotion to higher causes.

Eric Gill's memorial tablet to German graduates of New College, Oxford (1930). This exquisitely lettered tablet naming the three old boys of the college who died fighting for Germany in the First World War was a small but significant gesture of reconciliation.

Places of learning were important places of remembrance. The University of Leicester was itself a war memorial, founded in 1921. Winchester College (a public school) commissioned Sir Herbert Baker (1862–1946) to design a memorial cloister, around which the names of its 505 fallen old boys were inscribed; it is regarded as the largest private war memorial in Europe. Winchester's twin foundation, New College at Oxford, commissioned Eric Gill to create an exquisitely lettered panel with the names of its dead in the chapel; nearby, a small tablet records the names of three German-born college graduates who lost their lives fighting for Germany. It was a small but significant gesture of reconciliation.

Did you know?

There are peace memorials, too. Sylvia Pankhurst, the renowned champion of women's rights, was also a peace campaigner. In 1935 she raised a monument at Woodford Green (London), protesting Britain's failure to sign the League of Nations Disarmament Conference in 1932, which would have outlawed aerial bombing. The Anti-Air War Memorial consists of a stone bomb, carved by Eric Benfield (d. 1955).

6
Modern Times

For most communities there was no need to raise a new memorial at the end of the Second World War: all that was required was the addition of a new set of dates and the names of yet more dead, and add them to established modes of remembering. There had been a marked shift in popular preferences between the wars away from grandiose memorialization: cemetery monuments were becoming less assertive, and fewer public statues were being erected.

A Mass Observation questionnaire in 1944 asked the public about war memorials: 'Practically no one wanted the memorials of this world war to take the form they often did after the last – that is, costly erections in stone. Most people wanted "a memorial which would be useful or give pleasure to those who outlive the war."' Arnold Whittick's 1946 book *War Memorials* understood why a more practical form of monument was often preferred, but cautioned against puritanism: 'It is a materialistic and non-aesthetic attitude and has

Edwin Maufe's Air Forces Memorial, Runnymede (Surrey). Unveiled in 1953, this memorial to the 20,000 missing of the RAF consists of a cloister with a viewing tower or belvedere. It overlooks the meadow where the Magna Carta was signed in 1215.

little to do with the life of the spirit.' The reason for this preference was 'the failure of most of the stone memorials erected after the war of 1914–18 to express convincingly and in beautiful form what is commemorated'.

The biggest state investment in remembrance was the £50 million earmarked by Chancellor of the Exchequer Hugh Dalton in 1946 to set up the National Land Fund. Its aim was to buy culturally significant objects or places for the nation, in remembrance of the Second World War's dead: Dalton described this as 'a thank-offering for victory and a war memorial which, in the judgment of many, is better than any work of art in stone or bronze'. The National Trust was one of the early beneficiaries, but political unease about state acquisitions led to the slowing down of this commemorative facet of the Welfare State; its work was subsequently absorbed within the National Heritage Memorial Fund from 1980.

Nonetheless, monumental war memorials were created, some of which possess great emotive power. At Runnymede, overlooking the Thames Valley, Edwin Maufe designed the Air Forces Memorial, unveiled by the Queen in 1953. Over 20,000 men and women (including pioneer aviator Amy Johnson) had disappeared in the air war over Europe, and their names are recorded on the memorial's cloister walls; the viewing tower takes the visitor upwards to a fine view of the historic landscape of Runnymede, where the Magna Carta was signed in 1215, and upwards to the heavens above.

The Cambridge American Cemetery, Madingley (Cambridgeshire). Dedicated in 1956, this cemetery contains 3,811 burials and records the names of 5,127 missing, including Glen Miller's.

Other major commemorative sites were opened to the dead of other nations. The principal Second World War memorial to the American dead is at Madingley, 3 miles west of Cambridge. As it had done at Brookwood after the First World War, the United States Battlefield Commission created a memorial landscape of some grandeur: this contains 3,811 headstones, overlooked by a memorial chapel with a long stone wall inscribed with over 5,000 names of the missing. Inside the chapel are large-scale maps of the European Theatre of Operations and models of military vehicles: such factual elements were a feature of American military cemeteries.

The German Military Cemetery at Cannock Chase (Staffordshire), consecrated in 1956, brought together most of the enemy war graves on British soil from both world wars: these included shot-down airmen (including Zeppelin crews), prisoners of war and internees who had died in the Spanish Flu epidemic of 1918. Located on heathland, and planted with silver birches and heather, its landscaping has a suitably Germanic feel. So too does the gaunt statue of a dead warrior in the Hall of Honour. Just under 5,000 are buried here (including some Ukrainians). Just over 1,000 Germans from the Second World War are buried elsewhere in the British Isles, including on the Channel Islands.

Some conventional war memorials were erected after 1945. These included one to the Commandos at Spean Bridge, close to their training ground in the Highlands. Sculpted

The German Military Cemetery at Cannock Chase (Staffordshire). Consecrated in 1956 and completed in 1967, this brought together 4,929 burials from both world wars. The landscape was designed by Dietz Brandi in a fittingly German manner. (Wayne Cocroft)

Above left: Sean Sutherland's Commando Memorial, Spean Bridge (Scottish Highlands). One of the most rugged and heroic of all Second World War memorials, this statue commemorates the men of the Special Forces. (Wikipedia)

Above right: Christopher Webb Studio's Worcestershire Second World War memorial window at Worcester Cathedral (1952). Stained glass was a popular medium for memorials after 1945.

by Sean Sutherland in 1952, it stands over 5 metres tall and has the heroic qualities of Soviet memorials. Very different in character were the legion memorial windows installed in churches. Many of these display a lyrical tenderness and poignancy which is fitting for remembering young lives lost. Stained glass was a fitting medium for a modern memorial in an age which was increasingly concerned about the impact of new work in historic buildings. Hugh Easton was the artist responsible for some of the most prestigious commissions, such as the Battle of Britain Memorial in Westminster Abbey, unveiled in 1947, which comprised forty-eight panels depicting pilots beholding sacred scenes alongside squadron badges. Many cathedrals contain similar windows. At Worcester, for instance, the county memorial to its dead comprised a trio of windows by the Christopher Webb studio, painted in 1952.

Did you know?

The worst civilian disaster of the Second World War took place at Bethnal Green Underground station (East London) in March 1943. A stampede to reach the safety of the below-ground shelter led to 173 persons being trampled to death. A bold modern memorial was unveiled in 2017.

Harry Paticas/Arboreal Architecture's *Stairway to Heaven* memorial to the Bethnal Green Tube Disaster (2017). Britain's worst civilian disaster of the Second World War occurred in March 1943, when 173 were crushed to death. This memorial echoes the stairs on which they died.

Overall, the war memorials of the later twentieth century are remarkable for their modesty. Over 60,000 civilians were killed in bombing raids: their communal graves were marked by austere markers, naming the individuals buried below. At Coventry, the ruined Cathedral Church of Saint Michael, the victim of a devastating attack in November 1940, was preserved in its ruined state as a memorial. In other cities, like Bristol, Southampton, Canterbury, London and Liverpool, ruined churches were deliberately left as war memorials. 'Could there be a more appropriate memorial of the nation's crisis than the preservation of fragments of its battleground?' asked a letter in *The Times* in August 1944, setting out this concept. In the twentieth century, this battleground had reached the Home Front.

Above: The Second World War Civilian Memorial in the City of Westminster Cemetery, Hanwell (West London). Unveiled in 1950, this memorial marks the mass grave of 200 civilians killed in the Blitz.

Right: Temple Church, Bristol. This medieval church was badly damaged in an air raid in November 1940 and was left as a ruin: a number of Blitzed churches like this became war memorials.

Did you know?

The 1969 memorial to prisoners of war and concentration camp victims in Gladstone Park, Dollis Hill (North London), was the work of Fred Kormis. He had himself been a prisoner of war in Siberia from 1915 to 1920: his agonised figures were born out of personal experience.

The Second World War dead were recorded on existing war memorials, or laid to rest under the supervision of the Imperial War Graves Commission. As time passed, a new mode of commemoration arose: memorials to places, like aerodromes. While few of the memorials possess much aesthetic quality, they can possess an evocative power to recall momentous days. One such is the granite triangle at Polebrook (Northamptonshire), base of the 351st Bombardment Group in 1943–5, which states that 175 B-17 bombers were lost from this rural airfield. Another American memorial is the Sherman tank at Torcross (Devon), recovered from the seabed close to the scene of the 1944 Slapton Sands tragedy, when 639 men were killed in a surprise German attack; it was unveiled in 1984 as a memorial to all of the US casualties in Operation Overlord.

The fiftieth anniversary of the end of the war saw the emergence of a new genre of memorial: to the sacrifices of other Allied countries. One of the first was the monument in London's Green Park to the Canadian forces who lost their lives in both world wars.

Memorial (1981) to the 351st Bomb Group, United States Army Air Force, at Polebrook (Northamptonshire). Numerous modern memorials have been erected at former aerodromes to commemorate the men who flew from them, never to return.

This monument, designed by Pierre Granche and unveiled in 1994, consisted of a tilted surface, fractured in two, down which water runs over a poignant scree of bronze maple leaves, expressive of lost lives. Other Commonwealth countries followed on, with Australia and New Zealand erecting modern monuments at Hyde Park Corner.

War memorials had always had an international aspect to them: the dead so often perished overseas, and each war memorial brought to mind the sacrifices demanded of local communities by world events. No military memorial embodied this global outlook better than the Commonwealth Memorial Gates on London's Constitution Hill, close to the above mentioned memorials. Designed by Liam O'Connor and unveiled by the Queen in 2002, this tribute honours the huge contribution of the Indian subcontinent, Africa and the West Indies, and includes a memorial pavilion, Indian in inspiration, which lists the names of the seventy-four holders of the Victoria Cross and George Cross from these lands.

Recent monuments have sought to honour specific groups which, it is felt, have been hitherto overlooked. Best known of this retrospective group of war memorials is the Bomber Command Memorial in the increasingly crowded Hyde Park Corner. There was a strong desire to remember the heavy casualties suffered by Bomber Command in the Second World War. Over 55,000 men, some 44 per cent, had lost their lives taking the war to the enemy: no branch of service had a heavier casualty rate than this. Denied even a campaign medal, recognition was felt to be overdue. An elaborate monument (also designed by O'Connor) was finally completed in 2012, incorporating aluminium from a crashed Halifax aircraft in

Liam O'Connor's Commonwealth Memorial Gates, Green Park (London). Unveiled in 2002, this Lutyens-inspired tribute to the sacrifices of India, Africa and the Caribbean embodies the desire to widen the range of war memorials, beyond a purely British perspective.

its roof above the sculpted group depicting a bomber crew. One inscription refers to the victims of bombing as well as the airmen – an acknowledgment of the moral difficulties of the bombing war.

As the veterans of the world wars became ever fewer, so grew the appetite for new monuments of war. Run under the auspices of the Royal British Legion, the National Memorial Arboretum (near Alrewas, Staffordshire) provides a permanent forum for memorials that would otherwise struggle to find a location: growing anxiety about the profusion of monuments in Central London has made erecting further ones difficult. The arboretum was conceived in 1988 and opened in 2001. Laid out on 150 acres of former gravel workings, its landscape includes over 350 individual memorials. These range from Ian Rank-Broadley's Armed Forces Memorial (2007), one of the most ambitious of all recent memorials, to the poignant 'Shot at Dawn' memorial by Andy De Comyn. Unveiled in 2001, it comprises a marble statue of a seventeen-year-old soldier, blindfolded and awaiting death, surrounded by 306 wooden stakes, each with a name tag. It honours the 306 men executed in the First World War for cowardice or desertion – a hitherto overlooked group, who received a public pardon in 2006.

Who else had been overlooked? One of largest categories was that of women, who had played such a significant part in both world wars, but whose place in memorials had seldom transcended depiction as an allegorical symbol. Just north of the Cenotaph, in Whitehall, stands the 'Women of World War Two Memorial'. Sculpted by John W. Mills, and unveiled

Andy De Comyn's 'Shot at Dawn' memorial at the National Memorial Arboretum, Alrewas (Stafffordshire). Unveiled in 2001, the memorial remembers the 306 men shot for cowardice or desertion in 1914–18: it is surrounded by 306 symbolic stakes. (Elizabeth Blood)

by the Queen in 2005, its bronze form (echoing the Cenotaph nearby) is enlivened with hanging uniforms and work gear of the kinds worn by women. There are no bodies, only empty garments: a reversal of the muscular heroics which were long a mainstay of the heroic form of monument. Mills had made his name as a monumental sculptor with his 1990 piece beside St Paul's in memory of the firefighters of the Blitz – another class of wartime service which had not had the recognition many felt was their right.

Another overlooked group, albeit very different in identity, received a large memorial in London's Park Lane, not far from Westmacott's Achilles statue. This, the 'Animals in War Memorial' by David Backhouse, was erected in 2004 to the memory of the animals who had lost their lives in all wars. This was not the first time a large memorial had been raised to the memory of animals, however: in Lille, northern France, stands the elaborate stone monument of 1936 to the pigeons (and pigeon-breeders) of the First World War. When it is recalled that not a single private British soldier of the Napoleonic Wars received a public memorial, it becomes apparent just how far attitudes to remembrance have come.

Memorials are changing, as concepts of justice and historical memory change as well.

John W. Mills' Monument to the Women of World War II, Whitehall (London). Unveiled by the Queen in 2005, at the sixtieth anniversary of the war, this bronze monument celebrated the contribution made by women – a hitherto overlooked group.

7
What Now?

Further Reading

Alan Borg's pioneering *War Memorials: From Antiquity to Present* (1990) remains the best survey of the topic. For the emergence of the military memorial see Alison Yarrington's *The Commemoration of the Hero 1800–1864* (1988). Alex King's *Memorials of the Great War in Britain* (1998) is good on the social background, and Derek Boorman's surveys on the First and Second World Wars, *At the Going Down of the Sun* and *For Your Tomorrow* (1995), are full of interest. Gavin Stamp's *The Memorial to the Missing of the Somme* (2nd ed. 2016) is excellent on the Imperial War Graves Commission, and more besides. Geoff Archer's *The Glorious Dead* (2nd ed. 2016) surveys sculpted war memorials.

Useful Websites

The Imperial War Museum's *War Memorials Register* (https://www.iwm.org.uk/memorials) holds records for nearly 80,000 war memorials across Great Britain.

The War Memorials Trust's website (http://www.warmemorials.org) has much advice about protecting and understanding war memorials, and its *War Memorials Online* is a helpful illustrated index which reports on their condition.

Historic England has advice about caring for war memorials: see https://historicengland. org.uk/advice/technical-advice/war-memorials/.

The Public Monuments and Sculpture Association publishes expert survey volumes and much else besides: see https://www.pmsa.org.uk.

To find out more about casualties of the First and Second World Wars, visit the rich website of the Commonwealth War Graves Commission: https://www.cwgc.org.

The Battlefields Trust's *UK Battlefields Resource Centre* (http://www.battlefieldstrust.com/default.asp) contains much information on early places of conflict.

For exemplary regional websites, see the North East War Memorials Project at (http://www.newmp.org.uk/index.php) and Leicestershire County Council's survey, at http://www.leicestershirewarmemorials.co.uk.

Getting Involved

Established in 1997, the War Memorials Trust is devoted to the appreciation and protection of war memorials and welcomes new members. Local war memorials are generally in the care of local authorities: no work should ever be undertaken to a memorial without gaining the guardian's approval first, and any necessary consents. The War Memorials Trust's website is an ideal place to start. The websites listed above are keen to receive photographs and research or condition reports from volunteers.